REFLECTIONS ON EQUESTRIAN
ART

REFLECTIONS
ON
EQUESTRIAN ART

NUNO OLIVEIRA

Translated by Phyllis Field

J. A. ALLEN
LONDON

ISBN 0 85131 250 0

© English Language Translation
J A Allen & Company Limited 1976.

First published in France as
Reflexions sur l'Art Equestre
by Crépin Leblond 1964

First published in Great Britain by
  J.A. Allen & Co Ltd
  1 Lower Grosvenor Place
  London SW1W 0EL

1976.
New Edition 1988

Printed and bound in Hong Kong

CONTENTS

⁓✧✧✧⁓

Contents

PREFACE TO THE SECOND EDITION

Reflections on Equestrian Art was first published as *Reflexions sur l'Art Equestre* by Crépin Leblond in France, 1964, at the request of some of Maestro Oliveira's pupils. It was translated into English in 1976 by Phyllis Field.

Since then, Nuno Oliveira has taught in the United States of America and further afield in Australia and New Zealand. In 1987 he held a Master Class in England as a guest of the Association of British Riding Schools. Skill, artistry, total dedication and absolute brilliance have earned the Maestro international recognition.

Times change but classical principles remain the same. Over two decades have passed, but *Reflections on Equestrian Art* remains one of the most relevant and true descriptions of Nuno Oliveira's work. The publishers are proud to present this second edition.

FOREWORD

⟨⟨⟨⟨⟩⟩⟩⟩

Mr. Oliveira recently gave me several additions to his book which are not in the latest French edition, notably the Introduction, as well as an additional chapter on the trot.

I have tried throughout to render Mr. Oliveira's exquisite use of language into equivalent English which does not lend itself easily to the type of subtle circumlocution which is so delightful in the original, and often seems merely repetitive. It is also extremely difficult to have total precision while conserving the style, but I have tried to be exacting in that respect, allowing the language to become more plebian in favour of clarity.

There are certain untranslatable French words such as *écuyer*; to use trainer when referring to those erudite, cultured gentlemen would not convey the meaning of their role in the art concerned with the result of the horse's training. *Haute-Ecole, s'encapuchonner, descente de main*, and above all *ramener*, do not have English equivalents. I have, therefore, tried to explain their significance by using full sentences.

This book is unique as it is a simplified compendium of all the great masters' thoughts with practical possibilities of application today, as well as a revelation of the secrets of Mr. Oliveira's own methods which stem from his great

.ctical experience, in addition to his cultural and
olarly comprehension of the art which he has enriched
his own work.

Actually, at the date of publication of this English
edition, he has two horses in his stable, who are capable of
doing the Olympic Test in its entirety, including the classic
piaffer, with correct transitions to the passage and vice-
versa. He also has several young horses who are at a Prix
St. George level.

This will give some idea of his capabilities as a trainer, as
well as his renown as a scholar, making him one of the élite
in the horse world; an *écuyer*.

As a young man he worked as many as twenty horses a
day, while giving two collective lessons and some private
ones during the course of the day, starting his first horse at
four o'clock in the morning, and finishing his last lesson at
eight o'clock in the evening, both in jumping and in dressage. Today, he is uniquely concerned with dressage, training
seven privately owned horses in the morning before ten-
thirty, when he gives a collective class to pupils who come
from Asia, the United States, France, Belgium and England,
to ride at his beautiful farm tucked among the hills about
forty kilometres from Lisbon. He tends to the farm problems during lunch, and then from two-thirty until six
o'clock trains his own three horses, one of which he will
occasionally sell if he feels that a would-be buyer truly
loves the horse. Later on in the afternoon, he gives his
second collective lesson on horses which are masters of the
piaffer, passage or flying changes.

In addition, he gives clinics abroad, very enjoyable in
their country atmosphere and quiet comradeship, notably
those of Monsieur Laurenty in Belgium, where Mr. Oliveira
has many devotees, and that of Peru, where he goes once a

year. He will be giving several courses each year in the United States, at his riding school on the grounds of the Potomac Horse Center in Maryland, to further the pursuit of equestrian art. These trips keep his mind attuned to present day problems experienced by horsemen in all parts of the world.

Mr. Oliveira's wife is interested in horticulture and ballet and they have three children. The youngest boy is passionately interested in music, the eldest son seconds his father in the riding school, while their daughter studies art, in Belgium.

Opera is Mr. Oliveira's great passion, or rather it should be said, Italian opera, most especially Verdi, whose pure artistic life inspires him, and whose music resounds from the two riding school speakers out among the fields where the country people stop to listen as they till their fields, and tend their sheep.

PHYLLIS FIELD
Portugal
1976

LIST OF ILLUSTRATIONS

*It is rare to see a rider who is truly
passionate about the horse and his training,
taking a profound interest in dressage with
self-abnegation, and making this extra-
ordinarily subtle work one of the dominant
motivations of his life.*

NUNO OLIVEIRA

INTRODUCTION

⁓⁓⁓

"The horse is man's most noble conquest", the French writer Buffon remarked in one of his numerous works.

For centuries the horse has served man and has been man's best companion. Yet today, has he been forgotten and put on one side? On the contrary, in this modern world where machines and scientific inventions multiply unceasingly, the horse can have an important role. He is the ideal companion for man, who loves him and finds in his company something rarefied and transcendent.

For the young, the practise of equitation is a valuable lesson, as it requires the exercise of all human virtues. If they are introduced to the practise of equitation by qualified teachers, who have experience in this field, and above all, who love horses, these students can later cross the threshold and enter the domain of equestrian art, if they are gifted and passionate about it.

But what is equestrian art?

Equestrian art is the perfect understanding between the rider and his horse. This harmony allows the horse to work without any contraction in his joints or in his muscles, permitting him to carry out all movements with mental and physical enjoyment as well as with suppleness and rhythm. The horse is then a partner, rather than a slave who is enforced to obey a rigid master by constraint.

To practise equestrian art is to establish a conversation on a higher level with the horse; a dialogue of courtesy and finesse. The rider obtains the collaboration of the horse by the slightest hint of a demand, and the spectator can then see the sublime beauty of this communion. He will be touched by the grace and the form, and captivated as if he were hearing the most grandiose music.

Equestrian art has had its high moments and low moments across the centuries, depending on whether the age was one of enlightenment or one of materialism.

Xenophon, and before him Simon, coming from culturally advanced civilizations, have left us manuscripts, dated approximately 400 BC. These writings are filled with subtle advice, the base of which is that the horse must not be considered to be a tool, but rather a being who must be understood and loved.

The more barbarian, less refined Romans, have left no artistic trace behind them in this field. It is only much later, during the Renaissance, that Fiaschi and Grisone took up the artistic theme, followed by the French Royal Court who had a greatly enlightened sense of values in all the arts, which has given us Pluvinel, La Guérinière, and Nestier, among others. This period bequeathed to us a type of equitation which is the fruit of a time when beauty was the apanage and consequence of profound studies, and of a great love of all things.

This graceful equitation, characterised by its finesse, was later bastardised by the exigencies of war. That is why equestrian art had to be revived in its proper form by riders and scholars of genius during the second half of the 18th-century, as it had been made heavy, and thus mitigated, by military equitation.

In this day and age, the cavalry having been eliminated as a branch of the Army, rules have been established which permit riders desirous of studying equitation in depth, to be judged in competition. Some of these riders, but it is rare, attain the level of the true Art, while others, much more numerous, perform the series of exercises mechanically, while chasing after medals. The true rider feels for, and above all loves, his horse. He has worked progressively, remembering to help the horse to have stronger muscles, and to fortify its body, while at the same time developing the horse's brain and making it more sensitive.

It is at this point that a conversation on a higher plane becomes established which the horse will never forget, even if separated for a long time from his rider. He will reply to this conversation easily the day that he is reunited with his pedagogue.

Equestrian art may be likened to the construction of great edifices, which begun centuries before, are still far from being finished, built to endure in marble rather than in brick.

It would be inexact to say equestrian art stems from the equitation of combat. Over the centuries man has used the horse in war, and, as I have remarked earlier, it is only during certain periods in humanity's history that equestrian art is mentioned. This equitation, accomplished in beauty and grace, which was practised at Versailles, such as that of Monsieur de la Guérinière, was found to be inefficacious, when later tried by the army in battles against the Prussians.

In war the horse was used with harshness, by a man with the mentality of a warrior. In equestrian art the rider and the horse must have reached a state where all tension and contraction are eliminated, thereby establishing a deep communion by which a spectator, ignorant or not of the subtleties involved in this Art, but having a deep sensitivity, can appreciate this sublime beauty, in the same way he appreciates great moments in any artistic production of ballet, concert or theatre.

In the 19th-century, France had a genius in her midst called François Baucher. It is wrong to compare the Comte d'Aure to Baucher as Aure had a different aim from that of the normal *écuyer*; he wanted to write of, and to introduce into France, the hacking, hunting and point-to-point style of riding which the English had practised for a long time due to the gaits and type of their horses. As a result of this "Anglomania", Baucher had to use horses which were different from those types previously chosen, but he was astute enough to add to the enormous works of his predecessors, certain subtleties and intelligent methods which led to working the horse more lightly and intricately. The excesses which are found in his writings are due, above all, to the fact of his birth; of simple stock, he kept a rancour against the nobility who surrounded him in the practise of his art. In order to understand the feelings which animated him it is necessary to have trained many horses of all types, and to know how to understand all the philosophy contained in his works, while putting to one side the excesses produced by the prevailing social order of the times.

Must the rules of the *Federation Equestre International* (FEI) be held to completely? These hold that the Spanish Walk and Trot are artificial gaits, therefore not Classical, while considering that flying changes at every stride are quite natural in the horse, and nowhere give the great truism that, if the horse is well balanced and free from mental and physical contraction, all movements can be termed Classical. The definition of what is said to be Classical, has arrested all forward progress in this art by limiting the horizon to those who wish to study it more profoundly.

The apex of perfection in equestrian art is not an exhibition of a great deal of different airs and movements by the same horse, but rather the conservation of the horse's enjoyment, suppleness and finesse during the performance, which calls for comparison with the finest ballet, or performance of an orchestra, or seeing a play by Racine, so moving is the sight of perfectly unisoned movements.

This indeed is the true reward for all the work described in this book essential to the horse's training.

REFLECTIONS ON EQUESTRIAN ART

THE RIDER'S POSITION

Only a rider who has a good position may obtain valid results from his horse.

This position will be bettered when the rider's seat is as one with the horse, his upper torso enlarged, yet flexible, his legs well down, without being over tightened, while gently adhering to the horse.

The rider who is not properly in the saddle, supple, and as one with the horse can never achieve any independence between the various aids, a condition *sine qua non* to insure good hands.

It is only with a good position and a supple horse that the rider may succeed in stabilising his hands, thus being certain of never pulling on the horse's mouth.

A good piece of advice to all who want to ride well, and who wish to acquire a good position, would be to do gymnastic exercises; which give suppleness, ease and sureness in riding. The nearer the rider approaches an ideal position, the more he will succeed in difficult exercises without apparent movements or gestures, leaving the

observer with an impression of total harmony between
horse and rider.

THE AIDS

One of the key points of my preliminary instruction is
the entire relaxation of the pupil's legs. As for the hands,
the first care of a riding teacher must be to impress on the
mind of the rider that the mouth of the horse is sensitive,
and that to pull or take up continuously on the reins is
useless except to tire the rider, and make the horse insen-
sitive to a degree which stiffens him, and eventually makes
him almost impossible to stop.

Often one hears of an extraordinary rider simply
because he has good hands. Rarely does one hear of a great
horseman renowned because he knows how to use his legs
properly. Each one of these two requirements is equally
important to achieve fame as a great rider.

The rider's legs must adhere totally to the horse without
any muscular contraction, which will ensure a supple application of the legs when needed, and to which the horse
responds smoothly without either rigidity or harshness, or
in rejecting the action of the rider's legs.

If the rider who has his legs glued to the horse's sides
needs to touch hard with spurs, he will only succeed in
annoying the horse by tickling him in the ribs, and he will
never be able to drive the horse forward.

If the hands harden, they tend to keep the horse from going forward.

Only the rider who is free from any contraction will have a horse equally free from contraction. A team such as this is the ideal.

Students of dressage must be taught to use their hands and legs in a proper fashion, but above all they must be taught to use their head rationally when an equestrian problem arises.

TACT

There are all sorts of tact in the equestrian field; that of the hands, that of the legs, that of the seat, and, quite simply, the tact of the head.

The talented rider who is tactful will reward the slightest indication of obedience on the part of his horse, who will then respond calmly, confidently and pleasurably to any further demand. The true horseman should put into practice these words of Captain Beudant's: "Ask for much, be content with little, and reward often." (Beudant was an Honorary Captain of cavalry, and an author of various works on equitation, including *Dressage du Cheval de Selle*, Editions Berger, 1938, Levrault, Paris.)

A horse will never tire of a rider who possesses both tact and sensitivity because he will never be pushed beyond his possibilities.

27

In my Portuguese riding school, I once had a horse who did over 500 flying changes at every stride without being tired, obviously when ridden by a rider who was accustomed to those airs.

In order to train the horse to this point, I certainly did not over press him; on the contrary, I used extreme tact, knowing when to stop, when to reward, and when to ask for more effort.

Often it is tempting to force the horse in order to continue an exercise, or to place him in a certain attitude, without noticing that the horse resists simply because of physical deficiencies in conformation.

The successful horseman must make a study of his horse so that he may give lessons based on mutual understanding established gradually, and which will enable the rider to solve a fundamental question, that of the ideal position which must be given to the horse according to the specific exercise in question.

It is necessary to have great skill in order to arrive at this equestrian plateau. However, if tact is lacking, all the skills in the world are useless.

It is essential to have a sense of timing coupled with the knowledge of the precise method to be used at any given moment.

The person who loves horses, understands them and feels their needs, only he can have equestrian tact.

Some say that finesse in equitation is only for the pleasure of the rider, and that it should not be applied in the dressage of the horse, from whom is demanded a great effort.

I do not agree with this.

The greater the finesse of the rider, the greater must be his tact, thus obtaining results which enable the horse to acquire the most flexibility and mobility possible, resulting in a superior physical education.

Nevertheless, it is certain that in order to execute violent exercises the same finesse will not prevail as in a school lesson. A rider must have the greatest finesse possible, remembering that his attention is needed to resolve problems other than those given by the horse.

When I speak of a rider who has finesse, I am not speaking of one who does not help his horse, and does not maintain lightness or dash in order not to deviate from a totally perfect position which may impress the spectator, but which will not obtain the best results from the horse.

I have seen so many horses in competitions who performed as if asleep, the rider passively fixed in a good position, which is not to say I advocate a bad seat, or that a rider should mount in a simian fashion.

I most appreciate the rider who takes pains to render his horse light, insisting absolutely on impulsion, without the necessity to be tense, or to make great efforts.

The rider must try to get to the stage of always feeling, accompanying and aiding the horse's every step, movement or gesture.

When the rider's seat is sure, his legs well down, and when his horse attains a high degree of obedience and equilibrium, the rider will dominate without effort, and his stability of seat will be assured at all times without force or contraction.

It is this total ease and relaxation which makes the rider as one with his horse, without hindering any movement.

DRESSAGE

⌒⨦⨦⨦⌒

"Observe, and reflect!" (Beudant.)

I have made countless errors in the training of literally thousands of horses.

Luckily I am aware of these faults, for otherwise I would never have made further progress. I know that I still have much to learn, and will go on learning until my dying day, not only by riding, but by studying, thinking deeply, and observing.

The study and meditation of which the great masters have written must be carried out in the riding school, which is the equivalent of the architect's drawing board, and therein every good dressage trainer must prepare a programme in advance for his pupil, deciding one by one the steps to be taken in order to overcome the difficulties as they arise.

"It is the lightness of the horse which gives great cachet to advanced dressage, and at the same time expresses the indubitable talent of the rider (*écuyer*)." (General L'Hotte).

More often than not, it is we ourselves who keep a horse from performing an exercise correctly, and classically, by incorrect use of the aids, and by a poor seat.

THE HORSE'S MEMORY

The memory of a horse is astonishing and if this is ever forgotten by the trainer, there will certainly be great difficulties during dressage training.

Take, for example, the case of the horse who has a tendency to rush his fences. How many riders will have the sense to make the animal trot towards the jump, instead of continuing in a canter which will tend to make him overhasty?

I believe that a horse always remembers the last time that he has jumped as if it were engraved in his mind, therefore the last fence to be taken should be approached in the gait which is the most calm and most tranquil.

What value can there be in a new exercise for the horse if the demand is excessive? What end is gained in having obtained the execution of a movement if it is wrongly done, and if the horse is left with the impression of such a lesson? One cannot repeat often enough Beudant's injunction "Ask for much, be content with little, and reward often." In this last, lies the secret of leaving the horse still fresh, with a good impression for the next lesson.

A study of the memory of certain sour horses is most interesting and useful.

For example, when a certain exercise is demanded, which the horse does not like but which he knows will be asked for in a certain way and in a certain place, there will be more chance of success if it is asked for in that particular place and in that same manner than if tried under other conditions.

31

When a fearful horse is upset by a certain object, such as a vehicle, etc., and is obliged to pass close to the object of his nervousness by violent blows, his fear will never disappear. Each time he has to pass the object or place, he will remember the violent punishment and will again be upset. Instead, give him confidence and show him gently that he has nothing to fear. You will see that he will pass by it next time without the slightest nervousness, remembering your kindness in showing him that he has nothing to fear.

We must give all of our attention to the horse's memory which is a faculty of extreme importance in the training of the horse. Voice, rewards and caresses will stay engraved in his mind, and knowing how to use these precious adjuncts to the lessons of dressage is a proof of horsemanship.

LITERATURE

All books are of use to the very advanced rider who has had great practice in riding, so that he can pick out the good advice, using it profitably, while knowing which parts to discard.

Above all, it is necessary to ride often, while not entirely allowing the books to gather dust on the shelves.

SUBDUED HORSES AND EDUCATED HORSES

A horse may only be considered properly trained when by progressive and methodical gymnastics, without undue haste in the basic muscular suppling, he abandons himself to the rider's will without any revolt, assured that he will not be asked any movements which would be forced and would demand too much effort on his part. He will then work convinced of his pleasure, rather than in fear or apathy.

METHODS

It is only by rational and calm methods which are never brutal that the horse may become obedient and well balanced.

I cannot control my rage when I hear it said that the horse must be permanently pressed against the bit as this is the only way to vary the speed as wished, and the only way to have a completely straight horse. I would like to draw attention to the fact that there should never be any confusion between this heavy tension on the bit and the necessary light contact which activates the reins.

33

Obviously, results may be achieved by the method of pushing the horse hard against the bit, given a methodic gymnastic programme. But the same results may be better obtained, by relaxing the aids (*descente de main*).

In this system the training has been brought to the point where the rider's legs serve only to give the necessary impulsion to the exercise in progress, and intervene solely again when the rider wishes to go on to a new exercise. That is to say, in any gait the horse arrives at the peak of its ability and stabilises itself little by little until the trainer has a horse which will work by itself without continued intervention of the aids. This requires great sensitivity on the part of the rider, and clearly very sensitive horses. It is equitation for the élite.

By reading, riding, and meditating, great results may be obtained if there is a true feeling for the horse, provided the rider's seat is good, without following exactly all the details of any one method.

It must not be forgotten that there is no infallible method, nor a method that is completely bad, and that bad or good as these methods may be, it is in the end the rider who counts.

TRAINING THE YOUNG HORSE

It is a great error to use a bit in the first lessons. In such a case, resistance is almost always motivated by the colt's fear of the steel which has been put in his mouth. The best way is to use a normal stable halter with reins fixed to the sides.

From the very beginning what most matters is the instantaneous forward movement; anything deleted from the impulsion is bad for the progression of the training.

Using a whip behind the rider's leg gives a better result than using it on the neck of the horse, as many horse trainers do. Used behind it will activate the hindquarters, and oblige the hind legs to push the horse's mass forward.

Above all, during very early schooling the horse should stretch out and learn to have confidence little by little. It is only by giving mobility to the hindquarters, while disregarding the forehand completely, that the rider will feel that the young horse gradually finds his equilibrium, starting to feel confidence in the hands of the rider as he gently pushes his head forward, placing the base of the neck in a proper position as a result of the impulsion he has acquired.

To give the lesson of the spur to the horse, read General Favorot de Kerbrech on the subject (*Dressage Methodique de Cheval de Selle D'Apres les Derniers Enseignements de Baucher.* Emile Hazan, Paris.)

In brief, give the horse the habit of becoming immobile at the touch of the spurs. Once this complete immobility is obtained, depart at a walk, pressing with the spurs without relaxing the legs. This system accustoms the horse to have great respect for spurs, and to move forward instantaneously without hesitation or abruptness.

GIVING THE HORSE CONFIDENCE

Horses who have bad characters are rare; generally their vices are the result of inexpert handling by riders lacking in experience.

Supposing that a horse is frightened of a certain object and refuses to pass it, turning away violently. Is it punishment that is going to reassure him? I think not. All gentle ways are good, giving confidence and showing that there is nothing to fear. Punishing him would only lead to greater violence on his part. In order to train horses, a rider must have complete understanding of the subject. The horse must understand and accept any demand made by man without any resistance. Reward the horse each time he does what is asked of him. Never ask for more than he is capable of giving. Make him a companion, and not a slave, then you will see what a true friend he is.

ATTENTIVE AND OBEDIENT HORSES

A horse must possess superior impulsion to be considered really attentive and obedient to the aids. A horse may be considered attentive and obedient when he stays well balanced and is light on the rider's hand in the collected gaits as well as in the extended ones.

Generally, riders seem to forget that the basis of the horse's schooling is given by constant transitions and variations between gaits.

If the horse refuses to extend his trot, and instead breaks into a canter, he must be pushed energetically forward by using a direct opening rein with the aid of the leg on the same side so that he will have to move incurved towards the inside until he drops back to a trot. Thus, as he starts to trot again, he will be really in impulsion as the legs of the rider push the horse's mass forward.

When I say push energetically, I do not mean to make the horse's training exhausting for the rider. It is only necessary for the rider to know how to help the horse with the legs in such a way that there is little effort for both, so that there is real forward motion. Must we pass our existence at a sitting trot, kicking the horse with our legs, tiring ourselves, and tiring the back of the poor animal? Is it by trotting for hours with the horse's head at liberty that impulsion will be given to the horse? Neither one, nor the other; it is only necessary to know how to vary the cadence of the trot and to know how to rise at the trot. It may seem strange that I say that it is important to learn how to trot rising, as so many riders think that after the first lessons they know how to do this very well. Rising trot is not limited to knowing how to lift oneself off the saddle and to fall back in rhythm and cadence. It is necessary for the rider to know how to use the legs without effort or tenseness in order to push the horse forward while rising in the saddle.

It is vital that while rising to the trot the upper torso of the rider be not too far forward, and that it be kept at a constant degree of inclination. When the rider comes down into the saddle, the legs should greet the horse's body, embracing it in a forward movement.

I believe that, if from the start of training on through to the height of his dressage, the colt is urged forward, not brutally, but with gentleness, and without excessive demands which he would be unable to meet due to lack of gymnastic training, true impulsion will be obtained; which in equestrian art is synonymous with prompt obedience to the aids.

IMPULSION

Submission and impulsion are two qualities which are interlinked in the schooling of a dressage horse. The foundation of dressage training must lie in the perfecting of impulsion in the three natural gaits which become: the school walk, the school trot, and the school canter.

The school gaits differ from the natural ones by higher elevation in the horse's action, by their greater impulsion and by the rhythm and the cadence in their strides.

If the horse is worked conscientiously at the school walk, this will lead him to be able to execute all work at the walk with great impulsion, and great brilliance, while staying calm.

When, later on, an air of advanced dressage is desired,

such as the Spanish Walk, it will be seen that the horse will be able to perform it much more easily, with greater brilliance and exactitude, than if his schooling had excluded the perfecting of the walk. It is the same with the trot.

If the piaffer or the passage are obtained in any old fashion, profiting from natural tendencies of the horse, they will be bad exercises, detrimental to the horse. Often a horse will do them when excited without any demand being made, or else will produce them at the least pressure of the rider's legs. When a horse is able to execute the school trot in a correct fashion, he is ready to start these airs.

How many horses, when they do a piaffer are capable then of departing from this air into an extended trot and vice-versa?

In general, the piaffer, when taught by constraint before the horse is properly prepared, the rider profiting from the nervousness of the animal, provokes a loud clanking noise from the bit (the nervousness transmitting itself to the mouth), which is not a sign of lightness, but rather of sourness.

The relaxing of aids (*descente de main*) conceived by Baucher has nothing in common with fake lightness. Rather, it is the reward of superior impulsion in which the horse maintains his collection without needing the continuous aid of the rider.

A methodic training based on extensions and reductions of the gaits, during which the rider must see that the transitions are executed promptly, correctly, and gently, and based on making the walk, trot and canter while collection is maintained as the rider continuously urges the hindquarters to go forward, will prepare the horse to perform and perfect the most beautiful airs of dressage.

GENTLENESS

Is it worth while? Yes, always! Yes, it is worthwhile to "put on bedroom slippers" as Baucher advises, and to try to ride all horses, without exception, using the reins and the legs with the utmost gentleness and the least effort. We must not be deceived by the apparently rapid results obtained by the use of violence. Only rational gymnastics will solve any problems. Although far be it from me to say that there are infallible procedures for all horses.

In order to reduce to a minimum the problems and resistances which arise in the course of training the horse, it is necessary to have patience, gentleness, and some intelligence.

The horse will become accustomed to the aids little by little if you familiarise him with them gradually; thus he will be prepared for demands to be made on him, which will then become easy for him to execute.

I cannot stress enough, in the training of the horse, that the fundamental characteristic of his psychology is his memory. Although extremely useful in the horse's schooling, this memory makes any errors in training or violence by inexperienced riders infinitely dangerous. The horse will remember when he has been punished in order to force him to carry out an exercise that is uncomfortable for him, and each time that he is asked for that same movement he will become tense, and sometimes rebel in the expectation of punishment.

A horse is never trained by fear. Although progress may

seem slow, it is only by rational and gentle work that a horse can be called really trained.

APPROPRIATE HORSES FOR DRESSAGE WORK

If you want to shine in any branch of equitation you need to have a horse with good conformation, appropriate to the end desired. It is extremely important that the horse's character be good, so that heavy demands on him will not incite him to revolt, and that, on the contrary he will take it all in a good-humoured fashion. It can be honestly said that dressage, when properly understood, can change a horse by giving him a different balance from that with which nature endowed him, and in many cases, can cause considerable surprise.

Difficult horses are for the person who wants to go into equestrian art in depth, and who is really interested. But if the horse does not have certain necessary qualities in the role for which he is destined, no matter how long the training is prolonged the same satisfaction will not be given as with an appropriate horse.

WORKING THE HORSE IN HAND

Those who criticise work with the whip, and flexions of the horse's mouth while dismounted, affirm that when the horse is ridden, the weight of the rider modifies the balance, thus changing the horse's lightness. I absolutely agree with this criticism. When work is demanded at the halt, whether the rider is dismounted or on the horse, each time the horse displaces his fore legs in any direction outside the downward vertical line of the shoulder, he takes a position which will not allow him to go forward soon enough, and tends to render him sour. In lateral flexions the horse must stand completely gathered together so that no weight falls on the side of the flexion, nor on the other side. This type of flexion is only useful when the top of the neck is turned, care being taken to avoid the head going crookedly to the side, and assuring that the bottom of the ears are parallel with the ground. Dismounted work is extremely complicated, and I would advise any rider who is not well practised in dressage, or who does not understand it well, to avoid trying it. In any event, work with a whip is only a preparatory exercise done in the first phase of training. Advanced dressage must be carried out mounted.

However, I do not mean to say that when the horse executes airs or dressage he may not be corrected by touches of the whip. In the Spanish Walk, the whip's work is limited to obtaining the leg action. When the high leg action can be procured by the rider's hands and legs, the result is much more brilliant and exact.

PLATE 1

Harpalo Prince at liberty

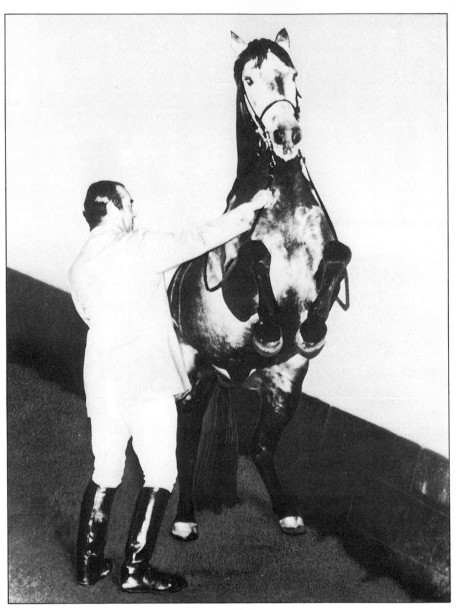

PLATE 2
Jabute. Levade in hand

FLEXIONS OF THE JAW

Not all horses need the gymnastic exercise of jaw
flexions. It is a waste of time to ask a horse who is well
balanced, who has a good lower neck position and a soft
mouth to do them. It is enough to mount such a horse
judiciously and methodically while working him gymnastically. These last are horses already born trained, and which
give worthwhile results easily.

On the other hand, there are innumerable horses who
will never be really light or capable of certain exercises,
even the most simple ones, unless worked with flexions
while dismounted.

Lack of mobility is always linked with the absence of
lightness.

Clearly it is not only by dismounted flexions that true
lightness may be obtained. Flexions done while dismounted are useful to conquer resistances or, I should say, con-
tractions of the jaw. If well done, flexions of the jaw are a
very precious aid during training of the horse. But it must
also be said that they are beneficial only when practised by
a skilled rider who is accustomed to doing them.

So many horses seem light in the riding school while
ridden at shortened gaits which have little animation, but
fall in towards the centre of the voltes, and do not
properly obey the rider's hands and legs when they are
asked to do more lively exercises outside.

The first requirement of a rider dismounted, when
asking for a direct flexion, is to see that the jaw is relaxed.
It is only much later, thanks to this previous demand, that

45

the horse may be asked to give way to the bit's pressure (*ramener*), without provoking any resistance.

To practise direct flexions by insisting first on the position of the hand and then on the relaxation of the jaw is to fall into the error of softening the horse's neck, giving it a false position which would justify the criticism of all those who disdain the use of flexions. If done incorrectly, the head position is obtained by force, which automatically presumes a forced compliance on the part of the horse. Horses thus flexed are only light in shortened gaits, and only then with great difficulty, while extremely heavy on the hand in extensions.

The criticisms of Baucher's flexions, particularly those of the contemporary German school, are erroneous. They are the result of a different conception of lightness.

HALTS — IMMOBILITY

In order to advance the schooling of a horse which has been given a certain degree of balance, it is essential to stop him properly every time a halt is demanded. He should not halt in a sloppy fashion, either stretched out, his head at liberty, or stubbornly hanging on to the bit. As he halts, his haunches must be slightly lowered.

At the halt, the neck must keep its correct posture, and when a direct flexion is properly demanded, the lower part of the jaw should show a slight relaxation.

There are so many horses who are not quiet because they neither know how to stop correctly, nor go from the halt to any other gait.

It takes tact and, above all, patience, to make a nervous and irritable horse stand absolutely immobile.

To begin with, neither the spurs nor the legs should be in contact with the horse's sides; nor should the contact with the hands be too strong.

What is important is that the horse halts and then stands still, neither incurving his body, nor fretting impatiently.

When this has been obtained (voice and patting help very much) the rider must try to make the halt correct, so that the horse is stopped by the rider's leg action which is followed by the intervention of the hands.

To accustom nervous and irritable horses to leg and spur contact, these last should be progressively pressed to the horse's sides, behind the girth. Then with spur pressing but not tapping, the horse should be made to go from the halt to the walk. This is to say that while keeping the contact of the hands, the pressure of the spurs, already in place, must be increased. Only when the horse has advanced one or two steps ahead can the rider's hands relax, and can the spur pressure be stopped.

This system gives magnificent results in dressage. Francois Baucher taught it and described it in his works on equitation.

During the course of dressage training, it is often necessary to return frequently to correct halts, especially from the trot. The transition from the halt to the trot, and from the trot to the halt, is one of the keystones of good dressage training, and makes the horse properly collected.

The horse must not halt with rigid hind legs, but rather by gently lowering his hindquarters in such a way that the rider feels this gentleness in the saddle, rather than a rough action.

The horse must not only know how to halt correctly, but must also remain motionless for as long as the rider wishes. Whatever may transpire, noise, movements, and so on, nothing should make the perfectly trained horse budge until his rider asks him to move. The rider must have a great deal of patience which will permit him to eventually obtain the desired immobility.

After the horse has been trained to halt, and remain immobile while alone, without other horses in the riding school, he should then be taught the same immobility while other horses surround him. Nothing should make him fret as the others circle near him, trotting and cantering.

I believe strongly in adhering to this minutiae of training. I do not think I am wrong to do so. In reading the works of the great masters, it is soon apparent that immobility and halts are problems to which they devoted much of their attention.

THE HORSE'S NECK; ITS PLACING, AND THE SHOULDER-IN

The horse may not be called submissive, nor in forward action, if the base of the neck is not in a stable position or

if the neck is too yielding, flinching from the contact of
the bit and the action of the reins.

Pulling the horse's head higher with the reins or carrying
out local flexions while dismounted will not obtain a high
carriage and stable neck position, although flexions are
extremely useful later in certain cases in order to achieve
lightness.

Activating and bending the hindquarters in gymnastic
exercises will stabilize the neck and give elevation to the
forehand.

The correct lowering of the haunches will provoke the
elevation of the forehand, never the contrary.

The exercise of "shoulder-in" correctly executed at the
walk, and above all, at the trot, will make the horse bend
and use the joints in his hind legs while causing him to
grow greater in the forehand.

I never begin the training of a horse by giving him a
lesson other than the shoulder-in. La Guérinière in his work
entitled *Ecole de Cavalerie* explains the position and the
aids necessary to achieve this exercise. In modern times, it
is not Salins, as many believe, but rather Gustav Steinbrecht,
as author, who gives the description of this exercise most
conscientiously and painstakingly.

The horse's legs must cross with clearly defined flexion
in all the joints.

Riders most frequently make the mistake of leaning
towards the inside. Amongst other inconveniences, this
loads the legs which are under the greatest strain. This may
be avoided by leaning on the outside stirrup.

Beware of the so-called shoulder-in, so frequently seen,
in which the rider pulls on the inside rein while leaning on
the same side, with his leg drawn back to jab the horse

with the spur, which forces the poor animal to move laterally while remaining twisted, and which takes all impulsion away from the horse, leading to resistance against the rider.

The schooling of the horse consists of a consecutive series of exercises in which, being sure of geometrical precision, the horse is placed in the right position to execute them. He must be placed correctly and left alone so that he can succeed. Once he is properly positioned, it is not desirable to continue giving the aids which direct the exercise, but merely to use those necessary to intervene in controlling the action.

All this having been said, here is the proper way to ask the horse for the shoulder-in:

Start turning a corner, having made sure that the horse is tracking correctly. At the moment when the horse enters the turn, the rider should turn his inside wrist, fingernails upward, towards the horse's outside shoulder. The rider's inside leg must stay by the girth, above all never going farther back. The weight should be on the rider's exterior buttock as the outside leg acts softly but firmly, a little farther back than the other leg in order to keep the incurvation and degree of obliquity required for shoulder-in.

When well executed, the shoulder-in gives great results as it eases, positions and straightens the horse.

Only when the horse knows this lesson well should the teaching of the half pass be started; this last, despite an analogous appearance with shoulder-in, is actually very different.

The horse must stay well in hand, and light as he begins the half pass, keeping to the same cadence with which he started, throughout the movement. Until the horse does half passes well, no other dressage movement can be started.

Having thus specified that the shoulder-in and the half pass are two totally different exercises, I must not omit to add that constant transitions from one to the other is one of the foundations of good dressage training, a schooling based on the easing of the horse, and not in making him more tense.

The horse being, for example, engaged in shoulder-in to the right, the right hand aids must remain in place as the left hand aids maintain the horse's incurvation in order to execute a half pass after the second corner of the riding school's short end. The animal moves by advancing from left to right. He must keep the same bend that he would have while doing a right shoulder-in, and he must advance, bent to the right, shoulders ahead of the hindquarters as a result of the enveloping action by the left rein. The rider's right leg should maintain the impulsion and the bend to the right with the help of the rein on the same side. The horse must keep to the same degree of obliquity with which he began during the entire exercise. The rider's outside leg stays in the same place as it was during the right shoulder-in, that is to say, a touch farther back than the inside leg, and should only intervene to give impulsion in case the hindquarters become idle.

This type of half pass allows the horse to achieve maximum suppleness and engagement. When the result is obtained, the half pass may be demanded with less bend than in the initial phase.

The degree of bend depends on the conformation of the horse. The more massive the horse, the more pronounced it should be.

The more that these gymnastics are followed, the more the horse will lighten, and the more he will become collected.

What is necessary in these transitions is that the horse be bent and straightened without losing a particle of impulsion, changing from one position to the other by use of invisible aids without alteration in the cadence.

To accustom the horse to change direction by an action of one sole rein, in conserving the bend to that side and then on the other side with the opposite bend, push the horse with two legs in these two positions, extending and reducing the gaits, while being careful of the transitions from one position to the other permitting a good neck posture and stabilising the base of the neck.

It is extremely important that at the outset of the colt's training he be left to take the head and neck positions which will favour development of propulsive force in the hind legs.

It is essential to make the position and attitude of the neck in accordance with the hindquarters.

In the horse's training all the horse's spinal column is worked from between the two ears to the tail's base.

If, because of a lack of proper gymnastics, the hindlegs are not prepared for the support of a raised head and neck, all the training will be compromised. All naturalness in the gaits will be lost and dismounted flexions necessarily must be practised with the horse standing still.

This work cannot be done in several lessons. It is interminable.

The hind legs are worked gymnastically, head and neck stationary while properly placed by correct flexions and the lowering of the hindquarters. Thus, certain difficulties can be solved by correct flexions carried out while paying

PLATE 3

Farsista in left shoulder-in at the walk, showing slight bend

PLATE 4
Farsista in left shoulder-in at the walk, showing a more
accentuated bend

attention to the correct attitude of the entire horse taken as a whole, ensuring that head and neck position will remain correct during all the horse's life, making him really light.

"The flexion of the neck, thus its permeability, may not be obtained except by impulsion propagated by the hindquarters which convey it on through the horse's body. These two phenomena, the compliance in the neck and the bend of the hindquarters, go together as a pair." (Hans Von Heydebreck, quoted in Steinbrecht's *Gymnasium des Pferdes*.)

Only with the greatest prudence can elevation of the neck be demanded while dismounted. Little by little, the horse's head may be raised without using force, so that the horse does not use his strength against the bit as his neck is raised. Make him give in to the bit in this position, and then, only then, allow the horse to bend his neck.

ON LIGHTNESS

The attainment of lightness in the horse is one of the aims common to all methods of every horse trainer. It is much talked of in equestrian literature, but in so far as all authors are in agreement as to its necessity, they differ in their conception of this quality.

For some, lightness means the absence of resistance in the jaw, and the positioning of the head and neck made sure of by semi-tight reins. For them, the horse is light when, accepting a gentle contact, the jaw gives way without weight in force. The horse, at this moment, starts to give in to the bit. For others, lightness is found in the horse's obedience to the rider's leg action, controllable by the hands which direct while not feeling any resistance.

As for myself, lightness is characterised by the simultaneous achievement of the following conditions: activity of the hind legs, and suppleness of the horse's back, both of which permit him to have, from the start of his training, a certain degree of collection, without making him give in (*ramener*) by the direct intervention of the rider's hand.

This kind of lightness can only be attained by a perfectly balanced horse. If the rider's seat is correct, his legs gently stretched down, his arms falling naturally, and his back completely free from any contraction, he will accompany the undulations of the horse's back giving the hands a degree of stability which will permit an assurance of the softest contact with the horse's mouth.

This true lightness is the one which assures the instant obedience of the horse at the slightest solicitation on the rider's part.

The attitude of the trained horse permits the use of semi-tight reins. Actually, the horse, schooled with maximum finesse, may be directed with the "reins attracted by the concept of gravity" as expressed by La Guérinière.

I believe this conception of lightness to be the stamp of superior equitation. It is a far cry from the methods which, under the pretext of making the horse taut like a bowstring, actually provoke and stimulate a constant traction on the reins.

Working in the pursuit of lightness, does not mean to work each part of the horse in an isolated manner, but rather all the legs, all the joints and all the muscles will function perfectly as a whole, because of the stability and complete lack of contraction in the rider.

RELAXING THE HANDS, AND THE LEG PRESSURE
(Descente de main et des jambes)

The horse having been collected, and having grown proud, while staying energetic and supple, the rider should then stop all action. The horse himself will make his rider release the hands and the leg pressure.

MOBILITY AND THE LIGHTENING OF THE HORSE

The difficulty in dressage training is the mobilisation of the horse, a gymnastic exercise which must be done in an ordered manner, without haste, as otherwise it results in nothing. If these gymnastics are done methodically, without haste, a great degree of mobility may be obtained; a mobility which will bring impulsion and lightness in its wake. Afterwards, the rest is simple.

The most complicated airs of dressage are not difficult if they are tried on a mobile, light horse.

In order that the rider may guide a young horse, who has rarely been ridden in a correct manner, the horse must be attacked (*attaquer*) in the croup area. This is so that the horse can acquire a certain amount of impulsion, and which will, due to the activity at the hindlegs, result in his mobilisation.

Once several side steps have been obtained dismounted and with the help of touches from the whip, do not insist by continuing on the same side. Go from one side to the other, often.

The trainer must try to make the horse walk with the least possible bend and obliquity in the lateral mobilisation so that greater activity can be obtained.

The constant use of semi-circles while the horse's haunches are held within, dismounted or on the horse, is excellent in making progress towards balancing and lightening the horse.

The horse must not rein-back in the semi-circles, nor should his croup escape to the outside; if in the dismounted work this occurs, the croup must be made to come back in to the circle by an opposing force on the outside rein, seconded by the whip.

In all exercises the horse must be given the clearest idea of what is expected of him.

Lasting impressions, from which stem submission, are the result of correct and fair actions, always the same ones. To speak clearly and simply always in the same way is one of the cornerstones of dressage.

The repeated usage of half-halts and halts from the trot is a great help.

Working the horse in circles is one of the most successful ways to give him suppleness, regularity and grace in his canter. The circular movement forces him to try to gain good balance, activates him, and places the hind legs under his mass.

As the horse grows more proud, harmony is established between the forehand and the hindquarters. When the horse moves easily in a circle at a walk, at a trot, and at a canter while keeping his hind legs engaged in action well under him, he must then be asked for the same gaits on a straight line; the rider being careful not to over restrain or compress him by the legs and hands.

All constraining exercises which give momentary fatigue to the horse should be followed by easier work, in which he moves without effort in his natural gaits.

The piaffer is not an end in itself which is taught as an adjunct to dressage training, but rather the gymnastic exercise which is most appropriate to perfecting and developing the gaits of a saddle horse. It is the best way to make the horse harmonious, completely subject to the aids, and submissive to the rider's will.

When giving a lesson in piaffer to a horse already familiar with this air, his strength will be concentrated more advantageously if it is demanded and obtained two or three times after each exercise.

In addition to calmness, lightness, and submission, which are desirable in all exercises, there must be added, impulsion and constant energy.

It is only in this fashion that brilliance, which makes a trained horse admirable, may be obtained, and it is only in this manner that equitation may be understood to be an extraordinary art.

A SUPPLE,
CORRECTLY WORKED HORSE

So many times riders attribute bad character to horses having a habit of rebellion, when often it is caused by starting certain work without sufficient preparation.

Training a horse is a rational gymnastics course.

So many times riders have the illusion that they have really achieved a predetermined end, obtained by their dexterity, tact and the predisposition of the horse to that end. When they perceive that these results are not consolidated, their recourse is to tighten the curb chain, lower the curb bit, the spur used to punish, etc. . . The horse gives way at first by good will because he is ridden with a certain dexterity, but when the demands continue for the specific exercise, an insufficient physical preparation does not allow him to work easily, without being tense.

The idea of ensuring sufficient preparation before any new demand is made on the horse, can be applied to the jumper, to the dressage horse, and in fact to all horses destined to be trained for whatever purpose.

The good rider is not he who, seeing resistances and serious difficulties appear in a new exercise, tries to conquer them at any price, sometimes using violence and

60

brutality, but rather he who, on seeing the resistance rise
up, knows how to return to the beginning, to the preparatory exercises, until he has obtained the flexibility and
relaxation necessary to start the exercise he is trying to
teach.

However, it is evident that having obtained the required
flexibility and suppleness, it is also necessary to ride with
feeling and even with virtuosity in order to obtain from
the horse all that he can possibly give.

"The aim of dressage training is to eradicate from the
horse stiffness in the joints, to develop in them flexibility,
ease in moving in a well balanced attitude in which they
can continue a long time, much longer than an untrained
horse, and with less expenditure of strength." (General
Josipovich).

FLEXIBILITY OF THE SPINAL COLUMN

The spinal column of a horse insures the liaison between
his forehand and hindquarters. In reciprocity, the hindquarters' activity is propagated by the intermediary of the
spinal column to the neck, the poll, and finally to the
mouth.

Because of this last, the muscles of the spinal column
must have supple tautness.

The spinal column must, of necessity, be strong in order
that the saddle horse may bear the weight of the rider.

In order to work the horse as he should be worked, with suppleness and lack of contraction, his spinal column muscles must not be over tense.

Tenseness in these muscles may manifest itself in different ways; certain horses dip their back, making a hollow in it. This is most frequent in horses with a long back, who often have badly set loins. Other horses contract the muscles of their spinal cord, humping their backs. This is most frequent in short backed horses.

I do not consider a horse with a short back the ideal.

The ideal back is one which is neither exaggeratedly short, nor exaggeratedly long.

The horse himself may be long without having a long back. What is most desirable is a long croup, not one that is short and swallowed-up.

The long backed horse, or one with an over long back, is generally the most comfortable. The concave back deadens the shock produced by the placing of the legs on the ground.

The short backed horse, on the contrary, is generally most uncomfortable. His convex back makes the rider feel more harshly the pounding of the legs.

A well conformed back, midway between the two preceding cases, can be flexed on two principal elevations: the vertical and the horizontal.

Dressage training seeks to give a horse which is not gifted with a magnificent back the vertical and the horizontal flexibility necessary to the harmony of the gaits and movement so that there may be suppleness and the minimum of effort.

It is these very muscles and joints of the spinal column that have to be watched with great attention during the training.

Each exercise, whose aim is to contribute to this flexibility, must be carried out with a head and neck position rigorously correct.

A shoulder-in executed with a trailing croup and incorrect incurvation of the neck only serves to render the play of the spinal column more difficult, and instead of harmonising the hind legs with the forehand, destroys their co-ordination. In this exercise extra care must be taken to verify that the horse's inside lateral leg is not more burdened than the outside one and vice-versa.

I believe that the attention of the rider should be fixed on the outside rein in a way which will complete and counter balance the effect of the inside rein.

Lateral flexions, a valuable means of bringing action to the spinal column, must be applied correctly. The horse must have his weight equally distributed on all four legs in order to begin lateral flexions. If this is not so, when the flexion is incorrectly done, and is demanded from the withers instead of from the poll, the back, because of taking an incorrect position, contracts and becomes hard, making the horse stiff and disobedient.

It is extremely important that the rider with refined equestrian sensitivity should discern the type of back of his horse in order to be able to make a judicious choice in the positioning of the forehand.

The condition *sine qua non* so that this positioning may be in harmony with the hindquarters, and with the horse's activity, is that it should be relayed by the intermediary of a supple and uncontracted spinal column.

Let us note with Steinbrech: "That for correct work, the conformation of the horse's back is of decisive importance, and that during training it must be the centre of attention."

THE REIN BACK

The rein back may be obtained after the horse can be collected in perfect lightness. It is unnecessary to teach the rein back. When the horse is balanced, light and relaxed, he is in a state to rein back at the lightest demand from the rider's hand.

The practise of rein back is useful for certain horses who push against the bit and who weigh heavily against the hand. Often, acceptable results are only obtained with these horses by making them back slowly, several steps while dismounted, the rider maintaining the position of the head rather high. Frequent repetition of this dismounted exercise gives good results with this type of horse.

It is indispensable during this work to maintain the straightness of the horse, and to make him rein back calmly and steadily.

If the rein back is rushed and precipitate, the horse must be stopped and asked to recommence in order to obtain the measured steps which are so desirable.

The rein back becomes a dangerous weapon if badly executed. If the horse reins back without being asked to do so, or precipitates his reining back, the exercise is bad, it even may be said to be terrible.

When the rein back is started on demand, and carried out without haste, it is a magnificent exercise which should be repeated frequently. How many times, with a horse having a tendency to be on the forehand, heavy and sleeping on the bit, would it not resolve immediately all these difficulties?

THE HORSE IN HAND
(Le Ramener)

One of the most famous authors of equestrian treatises, James Fillis, advised putting the horse in hand (*ramener*), by means of direct flexions, and with the maximum elevation of the head and neck, from the outset of the training. And one of the points on which he somewhat insisted, in the course of his works, is this one: "Push the horse well onto the bit."

The Germans also insist on the utility of sending the horse onto the bit, in order to stabilize his head position. Few horses, because of temperament, constitution, or sometimes because of acquired faults, tolerate this system.

I entirely agree that when trained, the horse must, on demand, go onto the bit, as it is commonly termed, but not by force.

After many years had gone by, Baucher, when comparing his first method with his new teachings, said to his eminent disciple, General L'Hotte, that now his legs were not as tired as they used to be. He gave his new method the name "equitation in bedroom slippers."

All horses cannot be given a head position bordering on the vertical. Certain ones can only be put in hand after great difficulty.

For some it is because they have badly attached and poor necks, for others because they have a neck position in reverse of the curve it should have, yet again for others it is because the neck is too short.

Horses which have very short and thick necks cannot be

65

light when in hand (*ramener*). Their noses must have a direction quite a bit above a vertical line dropped down from the poll.

The cases of horses suffering from loin, hock and back troubles, must be considered, as they are consequently difficult to put in hand. A horse with a defective neck always presents problems in his training, which takes a long time. Before having him, relatively speaking, in hand (*ramener*), he must be put through progressive and appropriate gymnastic exercises for a long time so that his muscles will develop in the desirable position without causing him to suffer.

Side reins are not, as commonly believed, infallible remedies in such a case. Abusive use of them will nearly always drive the horse into a form of stupor in which he will grind on his bit, and force the rider's hand.

If the horse cannot be kept in hand except by force and traction on the reins, he will be without gaiety, lightness and suppleness. If he is subsequently asked for lively and extended gaits, the difficulty he will have in using his neck will soon be seen, as will the lack of balance in his gaits. Instead of the neck extending, the head will lift up, star gazing and then the rider, in order to put him in hand, will start to pull on the reins. It will not be long before the horse becomes a real puller.

However, I do not want to say by this that side reins when well adjusted (not tight, not too loose) do not have certain advantages in the beginning of dressage training, but only as a way of establishing contact. Nor, also, that later they may not come in useful in order to confirm an already acquired position. But they must be carefully adjusted by a competent rider who has had practise in dressage training.

Generally the horse will oppose a resistance on the bit greater than that given by the hands of the rider.

It does not seem to me that what suits a horse with a concave neck best is to constantly pull on his mouth with the hands, or to ask for continued collection in an attitude of false lightness, which detracts from impulsion and balance. This is what most riders are tempted to do with this kind of horse.

This may seem to be the easiest procedure to adopt, but, in the end, it does not lead to anything. The horse may seem to go along very attractively and lightly in shortened gaits, but when he is asked for speed and mobility, all goes by the board.

With these horses, the fundamental work must include extensions and variations of gait, and transitions, incurvations and gymnastics applied to the whole body.

The action of the rider's hands must be of the softest.

The horse, through these exercises, will finish by taking contact with the hand, and will then be in hand. He should be rewarded right away, and allowed to move on a loose rein, as it is useless to keep him in an uncomfortable position which he is unable to hold without constraint.

Extraordinary patience is needed for this work. Obviously, this sort of horse should not be sought after for dressage.

Only riders having great practice, great knowledge, and gifted with great tact can train them.

Only these riders have the patience to know how to wait. Only they know that good lessons are followed by bad ones. They alone know that by patience and persistence they will win through. During a bad lesson, which is frequent with these horses before they are trained to a certain degree, irritation and force can only harm all that has been achieved before.

67

Tact and patience are indispensable. Lessons must be short. When the horse gives a little, do not ask for more, send him back to the stable.

A rider who becomes irritable, losing control of his faculties, can do nothing well.

There are riders who sacrifice lightness, suppleness and gentleness by not hesitating to use force in order to maintain the horse at all costs in a forced position. But they will only impose this forced position on the horse in reduced gaits. The horse takes control over the rider's force in extended gaits.

HORSES HELD
WITH/WITHOUT CONTACT

I regret very much that so many riders are not acquainted with the book *Extérieur et Haute Ecole*, written by Captain Beudant.

Therein it may be read that it is only by allowing horses to move on a free rein, and not in holding them in, that success may be obtained. Riders who hold in their horses are insignificant riders and will never advance.

Riders who give their horses freedom are those who will taste the delicacies of equestrian art.

WORK ON TWO TRACKS

The horse has not only the faculty to concentrate his strength, to collect himself and to cadence his gaits while going straight ahead, but he can also carry out movements to the side, crossing his legs and walking on two tracks which the masters of the French Old School called *chevaler*.

While walking on two tracks, the horse, in certain exercises, can be brought at times to cross his fore legs more, and at other times his hind legs similarly.

For example: the horse's croup, or more exactly one of his hind legs, is held in place in a certain spot and he rotates around this fixed point. Or, on the contrary, one of his fore legs is held in place and he rotates around this new pivot. In the first, he executes a pirouette, in the second a turn on the forehand.

While changing direction in two track work, the horse crosses his legs while advancing. The position and the rhythm of his movement must remain the same, from the beginning to the end of the exercise, the horse keeping to the same degree of obliquity. The horse's head must be lightly bent on the side to which he is going. During this light flexion, the head must not be crooked, the ears staying at the same height. The shoulders must not precede the croup in an excessive fashion, but it is a much worse fault to let the croup go ahead of the shoulders.

When in the volte on two tracks, haunches in, the legs of the horse make two concentric circles; the smaller with the hind legs, the larger with the fore legs. During the circular movement on two tracks, the shoulders must be always in front of the hindquarters.

69

The rider's inside leg takes the principal role in maintaining the impulsion.

When in a volte on two tracks, haunches out, the horse also moves in a circular fashion on two concentric tracks, but his hindquarters follow the larger track while the fore legs take the smaller track. Nonetheless, the shoulders must keep ahead of the hindquarters.

In any of the exercises in two track work, the rider must pay great attention to be in perfect command of the croup, sustaining or mobilising it at his wish. If the horse is left to take the initiative, the danger of his falling behind the bit becomes imminent.

If carried out with care, and with attention given to the forward movement of the horse, coupled with good collection, all exercises in two tracks are the basis of the horse's dressage training.

Future mobility depends on them. Hence take care to execute the work on two tracks correctly, never letting the horse fall into an incorrect position. In this lies the secret of the start towards good dressage training.

Only a horse which commences correctly will finish well. The merit of a good rider, and of a good horse trainer, is shown in the basic training correctly conducted.

THE SCHOOL WALK

The school walk is the natural walk at its maximum perfection, cadenced and well balanced.

PLATE 5
Harpalo Prince in half-pass at the walk

PLATE 6
Ousado in half-pass at the trot

The school walk takes different forms. The school walk of the old masters was a diagonalised walk in which the horse lifted his legs and collected himself. In fact, it was a preparation for the "gentle passage". The type of horse used, and quality of its gaits, led naturally to this form of the walk.

Today, due to the use of the thoroughbred type horses who have more elongated gaits and a head and neck attached less high, added to a natural balance which puts them more on the forehand than on the hindquarters, the school walk is in four beats, the horse elevating his fore legs as if in a parade walk.

For this walk to remain good, the horse must not hollow his back and give small, quick leg gestures like a majorette, but rather he should walk with a supple movement in the back and shoulders, putting his legs down as delicately as does a cat.

COLLECTION

The weight must be evenly distributed, the horse leaning neither more to the forehand nor balanced more on the hindquarters in order to be considered collected.

Essential to collection as well is the complete lack of resistances, as well as the maintenance of superior impulsion, and absolute submission.

The loins, hindquarters and hocks become flexible, the

hocks push the horse's mass energetically ahead as the movement of the shoulders becomes free and graceful. The head and neck are placed high, and the lower jaw gives way at the lightest pressure of the rider's fingers.

The horse should be so well balanced that the rider can ask any movement already taught with the minimum of effort, obtaining great promptness of execution.

I bow to the rider who, indifferent to his surroundings, works the horse to his own satisfaction, and having tried to attain his ideal, terminates the lesson, dismounting from his horse content and yet, at the same time, dissatisfied. Content because the work went well, dissatisfied because he feels his achievement to be far from the ideal.

DIFFERENT TROTS

In the gait known as the trot there are at least ten variations.

First there is the little trot, not necessarily collected, but rather a trot in which the horse is in a certain state of balance, not over exerting himself or using himself very much. This type of trot is used to relax the nerves while yet exercising an excitable horse.

Then there are two types of collected trot; one having a slower cadence as the horse is pushed on to the bit while yet remaining flexible, and the other having a cadence which is slightly less slow, with the horse's leg action becoming more pronounced and sparkling, but in which the horse is pushed less to go on the bit.

In the medium trot there are at least two more varieties than those of the collected trot.

There are three types to be found in the extended trot; the first being the one in which the horse extends his legs with the greatest energy possible without becoming necessarily completely rigid; another in which the horse is more relaxed, more giving of his back, and slightly less pushed on to the bit as he extends his legs to the maximum but more smoothly and softly than in the previous example, which clearly enables him to cover more territory; and third is the case of the extremely collected horse who throws his fore legs ahead while remaining totally on his haunches. This last trot is the result of the passage or piaffer.

Also, there is the skimming type of trot which becomes a vice in many horses, stemming from rigidity.

Finally, there is the working trot which the Germans use a great deal.

All these varieties of trot are obtained, not by the exclusive use of the aids, but rather by knowing the right dosage when demanding action from the horse's nerves; or, conversely, the amount of relaxation to the nervous system, which the rider must encourage at certain moments, applying his own actions, judiciously, in reference to the sensations that the horse gives him.

THE SCHOOL TROT

The school trot is the cornerstone in training a saddle horse. This applies as well, obviously, to advanced dressage training, if it is desirable to continue the training that far.

The school trot is characterised by a certain number of qualities: accentuated collection and elevation of the legs; carefully measured strides which are slow, high, and cadenced; full of impulsion which is much superior to that in any other gait.

In the school trot, the horse gains in height that which he loses in length of stride.

Joints bent, hindquarters lowered gently, the attitude of the forehand is high, and the lower jaw gives way to the slightest pressure of the rider's fingers.

When the horse has attained perfection in the school trot, and when he is capable of carrying out all the figures on two tracks at this gait, he is ready to begin the passage and the piaffer.

Many horses execute a short actioned trot which has nothing in common with the school trot. In horses, the slowing of the trot provokes precipitation in the strides.

It is a grave error, and it is the sure way for the horse, who does not like to go on, to hold himself back and to become sour.

The more the horse is collected in the trot, which he becomes by infinitesimal degrees, lesson by lesson, the more slow and cadenced is his gait.

The shoulders being free, which allow the fore legs to be lifted, the correct flexion of the hindquarters makes the hind legs enter under the mass, and as a sign of impulsion the hind fetlock is in contact with the ground.

A good school trot can only be attained if, right at the beginning, there has been adequate gymnastic training which gives suppleness to each hind leg, one by one, so that the equal flexion and activity of each one has been put in a state to work at a trot in such a fashion that they

PLATE 7
Farsista in extended trot

PLATE 8
Corsario ridden with a string in his mouth at the passage

can push the horse's mass ahead in an absolutely equal way.

Therein resides the crux of the problems met in trot gymnastics.

Half a resistance, even a quarter of a resistance, in the hind legs at the trot is enough to compromise the ensuing lessons at the trot.

If, at a shortened trot, there is one diagonal almost inactive, a diagonal which is retarded, it is because the corresponding hind leg to this same base diagonal is offering resistance, does not bend, and hence is not activating the horse's mass in the same manner as its neighbour.

Working in a circle which will force the hind leg more into use, half shoulder-in, and in certain cases, counter canter, are methods to employ in order to solve these problems. For example, if the left hind leg is somewhat inactive, the horse must be made to go to the right in counter canter (being on the left lead).

It is only after having obtained equal work from the two hind legs, that is to say, having assured the rectitude of the horse, the collection, at the trot, little by little, can be increased.

In the measure that the horse maintains collection in the trot with less and less effort, the hands and legs of the rider can relax, allowing the horse to continue by himself in a gait and in a state of balance which pleases him.

Light brushes with the spurs, coupled with perfect dexterity of the hands, give height and a cadenced gait to the trot, which will constitute the school trot, as soon as the suspension and placing of the diagonals are perfectly correct and harmonious.

When the horse has attained this degree of perfection, he may start to be taught the airs of *Haute-Ecole*.

The passage and piaffer cannot be correct and academic until the horse has been prepared in a good school trot.

"The school trot renders the horse supple, attractive, light and, in one word, puts him in perfect balance." (General Decarpentry)

EXTENDED TROT

The extended trot can only be obtained through extreme impulsion. For this to be true, it must be executed from the peak of collection in the school trot. It must be ample, and must not include any harshness or precipitation in the gait.

Even at the maximum extension of the trot, the horse must keep his legs supple. The movement must not be rough. The so-called extended trot, in which the horse stiffens his back, gesticulating with his lower front legs as if "shooting his cuffs", pulling on the reins below a rider who uses his legs at every stride cannot be considered as being in the domain of impulsive, classical equitation.

The true extended trot is the one which is the result of maximum impulsion in collection.

During the last strides of cadenced trot, passage, or piaffer, the rider, by opening his fingers, allows the horse to extend.

The animal needs no pushing, his back stays flexible, his hind legs well engaged under him and detaching themselves from the ground, his fore legs sent well ahead, as their movement leaves the shoulder and goes right to the front of his shoe.

The horse should not throw out his legs towards the ground, but rather stretch them forward, as if he were trying to reach the farthest distance possible with his feet.

Obviously, the attitude of the horse in the extension differs according to his degree of training.

The horse can extend his neck as he extends the trot in a horizontal state of balance.

In a collected state of balance, the horse should hold the same neck position in the extension as has previously been obtained.

THE PASSAGE

When the horse has been advanced enough in his dressage training so that he remains well balanced in all three gaits, he is ready to be taught the passage, or the piaffer.

The school trot is the basis for instruction in the classical airs of the *Haute-Ecole*.

To quote Gustav Steinbrecht: "Only the horse which can execute the lessons of the trot with surety and perfect ease is sufficiently prepared for the passage, and may be advantageously worked therein."

When the horse has attained maximum lightness and impulsion in the school trot, he goes naturally into the passage, almost by himself. Then the rider's work must consist of regulating the passage by total co-ordination of his leg actions with those of his hands.

Good dressage lies in the concordance of the aids.

It would appear that I believe that the passage and piaffer are easily obtainable from all horses. Far be it from me to have such pretensions. I have taken terrible pains to obtain these airs from certain horses who had extreme difficulty in learning them.

What I do say is this: the easy thing, actually very easy, is to obtain something of these two airs when there has been success in making the horse execute the school trot in perfect and constant collection.

It is this collection that is difficult to obtain from certain horses.

There are different kinds of passage, depending on the conformation of the horse, and the style of his gaits.

A very high passage is brilliant, but it is not the height of the action which indicates the quality of the passage. It is rather the slowness, tied to the time of suspension.

The diagonal which has just touched the ground must begin to detach itself with energy before the other diagonal starts to descend again.

The better a horse is muscled and suppled, the better will he achieve a maximum amount of grandeur in the passage. As well, in order that the passage can be slow, and so that the horse marks the suspension time for as long as possible, all the joints must be well flexed.

The engagement of the hind legs in their work at the passage depends on the style of their action in a natural trot.

There are those horses who raise their hind legs by bringing up their hocks and flexing their fetlocks without

PLATE 9
Maestoso Stornella piaffer in long reins

PLATE 10
Talar in piaffer

advancing their legs under their body. Other horses, on the contrary, while flexing the joints less, advance their legs under their body to an excessive degree.

These two styles of hind leg engagement correspond to a more pronounced bend of the hindquarters in the first case, less pronounced in the second.

As to the fore legs' action, passages in which, at the moment when the forearm is at its highest point while the cannon of the fore leg supporting the weight is *very slightly* above or below the vertical, cannot be considered necessarily bad.

All this stems from the horse's natural way of moving. The important thing, as Captain Beudant has said so precisely, is that "the movement be rounded."

Energy due to impulsion and amplitude because of strength are a necessity in order to make *Haute-Ecole* a spectacle of beauty.

My master, Joaquim Gonçalves de Miranda, executed some passages with his horses which are engraved on my memory. I have seen few comparable since then.

"The horse must be given all the brilliance which lies within him." (Beudant)

PIAFFER

A slow and high piaffer is very difficult to obtain; all horses will not stand up to it. I think it is the keystone to *Haute-Ecole*.

The horse must be taught to piaffer, by calming him, and not by exciting him. According to the temperament of the horse to be trained to piaffer, there are different methods of teaching it.

With an energetic horse, having steady gaits and a natural disposition to collection, it is wiser to teach the passage first, and then when this is really correct, to shorten it little by little until it becomes a piaffer.

In this way, a tendency to go immediately into a diagonal movement, and to be impatient when a halt is called for, is avoided, a habit which is almost inevitable when the piaffer is taught previous to the passage.

It is necessary, and very important, as in the passage, that the horse should not be excited by the piaffer, so that his walk, this precious attribute which must not be neglected at any moment during his education, does not lose its regularity or become soured.

Given an energetic, but calm, horse who has little tendency to fall into a diagonal movement, I think it preferable to teach the piaffer first. As soon as the piaffer is nice and slow, well cadenced, and the two beats rigorously equal and synchronised, he can be pushed forward little by little, and he will go into the passage.

In order to obtain the piaffer with this second type of horse, I think it advisable to follow Steinbrecht's counsel in *Gymnasium des Pferdes*: have the horse easy to halt and to start in immediate departures at the trot; methodically, little by little, reduce the strides of the trot between the halts, until the horse starts to piaffer. It is very important with this system to maintain the horse rigorously straight in all the exercises.

With a lethargic horse who has less impulsion, and not much aptitude for collection, the piaffer is difficult to

PLATE 11

Impostor in piaffer

PLATE 12
Corsario in Spanish trot

teach, but extremely useful for his dressage training, and eventual usage.

This sort of horse must be started from a halt, while provoked little by little, without forcing him, into a light mobilisation, but not while advancing.

When this mobilisation comes easily upon the demand of the rider, who should use the spurs very lightly far back as if he were pinching a guitar string, without any leg pressure and with the aid of the tongue, the whip gently brushing the sides of the animal in spaced out taps, then this precipitation and mobility in place, will be transformed into the piaffer. As soon as this piaffer is really a piaffer, he must be asked to advance in order to transform it into the passage.

There are horses for whom transitions from passage to piaffer and from piaffer to passage present enormous difficulties, which calls for great tact and finesse to resolve. The reason for this is that during a certain time they are not executing correctly one or the other of these airs. Once the execution is good, the transition will come.

I recall the good advice that Favorot de Kerbrech used to give, concerning a horse with a croup that deviated from the straight, during the piaffer. He corrected it "by a seesaw effect of the hand, from right to left, left to right with a sort of pliant and steady vibration."

In order to correct a piaffer in which the horse has his fore legs too far under him, it is necessary to go back and practice the school trot with frequent halts.

The piaffer will then begin to take form if the halts are done with correct flexion of the hindquarters and enlargement of the forehand. As the forehand rises correctly, and as the action of the fore legs becomes slow and high, the horse finds the right balance point in the supporting fore leg.

When the horse knows how to piaffer, he can begin any other gait without hesitation or effort.

THE SPANISH WALK

Included in the French equitation of a century ago are several valuable gymnastic exercises, such as the Spanish walk and trot, which German critics of the time and other so-called purists called artificial airs.

I have seen, quite recently, a young horse who, newly arrived from the pasture, and let loose in the indoor riding school did some steps of the Spanish walk naturally, stepping very high and brilliantly. This is my retort to those who denounce as artificial the magnificent exercises of this type of equitation.

I do not consider these two latter airs difficult to teach, and, I consider them a useful gymnastic exercise for any horse, without exception, believing them to be valuable auxiliaries in the task of giving mobility and elasticity to horses.

In order that they may be beneficial, they must be executed in a well balanced attitude, the horse at ease, and it must be remembered that the Spanish walk, like a normal walk, consists of four equal beats, and the Spanish trot of two beats, perfectly connected diagonally as in the normal trot.

So many problems may be resolved by a Spanish walk

judiciously used, and at the desired height. For example: a horse who has a very high croup and a timid stride in the fore legs which restrains that of the hind legs, will be helped by the gymnastics of the Spanish walk.

It can also help the horse, who because of bad dressage training, has defective collection, his fore legs being too far underneath his body. In such a case the Spanish walk gives amplitude to the action of the fore legs, modifying little by little their defective attitude until it becomes correct.

How should the horse be initiated into that air? It is obvious that it should only be undertaken with an obedient horse, who responds well to the leg and hand actions of the rider. Generally, it is better to begin this lesson dismounted.

The horse must be placed next to the wall, very straight (this last is extremely important) and at a rigorously imposed halt. An indication should be given with the snaffle rein on the side of the fore leg desired to be the sustaining one, this being necessarily the interior leg, without permitting any tendency towards a shift of weight to the rear, and then the rider should start to touch the previously mentioned fore leg with the whip.

According to the horse's reaction, it is necessary to touch him with the whip in different areas, until a slow elevation and calm replacement of the fore leg has been obtained.

In the beginning, the horse cannot be expected to lift and replace the fore leg without bending the knee. The important point is to pat him immediately when he starts the action of the Spanish walk, whether it be high or low, so long as the horse remains calm and straight.

The whip may be used to touch the area from the elbow to the fetlocks until the place is found where, when touched, the horse reacts the most, causing him to extend his fore leg to the maximum.

It is very important not to lose contact with the opposite side to that which the snaffle rein is helping, nor to have any lack of the pressing rein of opposition which is a condition *sine qua non* to ensure the maintenance of an absolutely straight horse, and equally important not to overload the shoulder from which the action is asked, as this would render this movement difficult.

As soon as the horse extends his fore leg at the lightest touch of the whip; the way in which he thrusts this fore leg forward while extending it, as if he were trying to seize an object out of reach, should be studied and determined. When this is obtained, he must be kept at a walk in which the fore leg touched stretches out into the action of the Spanish walk, while its neighbour is put down as if at a normal walk.

When the horse executes this walk without difficulty, both sides alike, this phase of dismounted work is finished.

The first mounted lesson must be given with the same care regarding the calm and rectitude of the horse, as was demonstrated during the dismounted part.

Using a long whip alongside of his shoulder, held with the rider's hands high, the horse must be touched on the fore leg until it extends. Pat him immediately, and do one or two circuits of the riding school at a free walk. Stop at the place where he has given the action, and ask for it again. When the horse does it easily, upon the approach of the whip, begin to associate this approach with an indication by the direct rein, used in a continued low to high movement by the hands.

Little by little the horse will understand what is asked of him, and the use of the whip may be abandoned. However, I do not advise discarding it totally as, if the action does not come easily, or is not high enough it can be usefully employed in case of need.

When the high gesture of the fore legs is given easily on demand with both legs, begin to ask for the walk with the high action on the side nearest the wall only.

When the horse can carry out this walk while keeping himself straight, ask for the same walk but this time with the gesture given on the inside only.

When the horse can execute, for example, four or five steps of the walk with a high gesture on one side, and then four or five steps with an equally high gesture on the other side, alongside the wall while keeping calm and straight, he is then ready for anything which may be asked of him including two or three consecutive complete steps with high gestures from first one and then the other fore leg which constitute the Spanish walk.

"Ask often, be content with little, reward largely."

Never demand more of a horse than that which he is ready to give.

It is very important that the horse puts down his fore feet lightly (not striking the ground with force, which would only show that he is not calm) during the Spanish walk.

The air may be considered correctly done when, responding to very light indications of the rider's hands and legs, the horse raises and extends his fore legs, without altering the rhythm or the cadence of the ordinary walk.

Even though today many consider the Spanish walk to be a circus air, the way of obtaining it which I have just explained seems to me to contradict this opinion, as it calls for procedures of training which do not extend out of equitation's domain.

"The height, the extension and cadence are the qualities

93

which give the Spanish walk its value." (D. José Manuel da Cunha Menezes)

If well done, with good carriage of the head and neck, without alteration in the walk, it is an elegant spectacle, and a healthy gymnastic exercise. It is beneficial, favouring a great development of the shoulders, and amplification of the fore legs' stride. It makes the horse mobile, elastic, and brilliant when coupled with the gymnastic exercising of the hindquarters.

SPANISH TROT

This gait is a trot in which the horse raises, and holds steady for an instant, the fore legs, while extending them. In the Spanish trot, the horse must stay calm and cadenced, and when he puts his fore feet down, it must not be in a harsh or nervous manner, but rather softly and energetically.

If the horse executes the Spanish walk well, the way to ask for the Spanish trot, and the procedures to follow are:

Imagine, for example, at the instant when the right fore leg is extended, the horse is touched strongly by the left spur, making him take a small leap forward. This is the first step. Do not ask for more and do reward him.

Begin all over again and when the first step is really assured, ask for the same thing while the left fore leg is extended.

When the first step has been obtained with each fore leg,

PLATE 13
Impostor in passage

PLATE 14
Zurito in canter to the rear

the horse may be asked for two, but only after the isolated steps have been correct in their height, cadence and stability, and are done with ease.

If the horse tends to be more lazy in one fore leg action than in the other, work the difficult one by itself.

When harmony has been established, link the two first steps, continuing until four have been given, without asking for any more over a long period even if the horse would like to do more.

This is a way of ensuring the height and stability of the Spanish trot.

It is very simple to teach the Spanish trot if the horse does a good passage which is energetic and well impulsioned, and I believe that if this is the case, provided enough tact is used, the horse will come to do it with rare brilliance and with the fore leg marking a long time in suspension. In this instance, the instruction in Spanish walk becomes unnecessary. It is sufficient to teach the horse the high leg gesture which should soon be done with ease.

Put the horse into a passage and by diagonal aids make him execute the high leg gesture while continuing the passage near the wall. Stop and reward him.

Ask for the same thing on the other hand.

When all that has been taught, and is easy for the horse make him do several high leg gestures with the same fore leg, interspersing them with steps of the passage on the other side. Start to ask for isolated steps with the inside leg, and as soon as the horse can do five or six strides to the right, and five or six to the left energetically, without becoming incurved, reward and stop him. It is then time that he be asked for the two steps in succession, one to each side, which constitute the beginning of the Spanish trot.

Help the horse by using the spurs well in front of the place that they usually touch when the passage is demanded, and raise the hands high, so that the horse does not confuse this air with the passage.

If it seems desirable to teach the horse various airs, a gradation in the placing of the spur on the flanks will have to be established, localising the touches according to the pre-determined exercise. This area of gradation should be located near the girth, one, but never more than two, hands width behind it.

The rider's legs must be well down, which is the only admissible position in order to be correctly seated on horseback. Only he who has given his horse a good head and neck position will succeed in executing the airs of the *Haute-Ecole* easily, and without annoying the horse with useless and unsightly movements.

In this system of training in the Spanish trot, if the horse should refuse to lift one of his fore legs, he must be stopped, and asked to give the high leg action on this side, and then he must be made to go into the passage, while being obliged to execute the high leg action at that gait by means of a light rein action, lifted from a low position to a high one, on that same side.

I think that if it is not overdone, the horse will quickly understand what is wanted of him.

With certain horses it is necessary to teach the Spanish trot before the passage. Be that as it may, if the horse is taught the passage first, he is in better muscular condition and gymnastic training to begin a more effortless Spanish trot.

The transition from passage to Spanish trot, and vice-versa, is a very valuable exercise, and a beautiful sight to see.

I close on that note with a word of advice: the air should be done only with strong and well made horses who have legs that are in good condition.

WORK AT THE CANTER

The typical canter is a rising gait of three successive beats, in which the simultaneous setting down of the two legs composing one diagonal takes place between the successive setting down of the opposite two legs.

The over anticipated setting down of a fore leg, in one diagonal pair during the canter in three beats time, will lead to a canter in four beats time, as the horse puts himself on his forehand.

The over anticipated setting down of a hind leg, will lead to canter in four beats time on the haunches.

The first lacks amplitude and impulsion; it is unattractive and rough.

In the second instance, the horse is on his hindquarters, and takes on a majestic air.

This is the gait of the canter in place, the canter to the rear and the canter of the pirouette.

THE STRIKE OFF AT THE CANTER

The way in which the strike off at the canter should be done has been the object of innumerable controversies.

The Comte d'Aure provoked the strike off at the canter to the right by using his left leg, after having slightly turned the horse's hindquarters to the right by employing the left rein.

Baucher, in his first method, used diagonal aids. His example was followed by James Fillis, and by nearly all the *écuyers* of that time. But at the end of his career, Baucher finished by using interior lateral aids.

Each one of these ways is good. The most essential thing is to give the horse the appropriate gymnastic preparation in order to strike off in the canter by pre-determined aids.

The horse must be well impulsioned, and well cadenced at a canter in three beats time, and he must hold himself straight on each hand, (this is the most difficult thing for a horse) before he starts to do flying changes or pirouettes.

One of the most beneficial exercises for obtaining flexibility, straightness, and unification of the forehand with the hindquarters, is the shoulder-in at the canter, along the side of the wall.

Half halts done with tact, after having made sure that the horse is completely straight, rein back, and strike offs at the canter without any brusque movement, are all excellent exercises.

Frequent strike offs at the canter, coupled with relaxation (*descente de main*) of the aids which do not modify in any way the attitude, nor the cadence of the canter, are highly recommended: the relaxation (*descente de main*) of the aids acts as both a verification of the degree of collection attained, and as a reward.

A horse is not taught balance at the canter by cantering for a long time, but rather by doing frequent strike offs from the walk and from the halt.

The acme of dressage training is work at a canter, brought to perfection.

However, it is not advisable to begin flying changes before the horse can maintain the counter canter in a circle effortlessly and without losing collection.

COUNTER CANTER

Counter canter is an extremely efficacious procedure in dressage training, and is an extraordinary preparation for the collected canter. If it is done on the outside track of the riding school, the wall will stop the croup from escaping, preventing the horse from refusing to flex the inside hind leg (in the context of the canter) by making a barrier against the lateral deplacement of the croup.

The rider can pay attention in the regular canter to the maintenance and flexion of the inside hind leg, as he has the wall to control the outside hind leg.

More attention should be paid to the outside hind leg (according to the canter) in the counter canter whose activity favours at the same time that of the inside hind leg.

We can cadence the gait, activate it, make it rounder, and transform it into a canter with greatly superior impulsion by means of the counter canter, without fear of making the horse crooked.

At the outset, the counter canter is a violent exercise for the horse. It must not be overdone, as then instead of having a beneficial effect, it will come to have a harmful one. The counter canter should not be started until the horse can stand a certain amount of collection.

The horse's collection will be activated and perfected by the counter canter.

When circles in counter canter are started, the croup pushes the horse's body energetically because of the position of the two hindlegs, which are necessarily flexed and activated strongly.

So many riders think that counter canter, and circles in the counter canter, are unnecessary, alleging that when a volte on two tracks at the canter is asked for, it should be done in a confined space, so that the forehand turns around the croup rather than the opposite.

They forget that the croup cannot stay in place and in a lowered position unless it has been previously mobilised. It is the counter canter which gives mobility to the croup, by activating the hind legs.

Counter canter, above all in the corners, is difficult at first for many horses.

If, at the corner, the horse changes lead, leans toward the inside, or becomes disunited, he should be stopped and collected in order to strike off again in counter canter.

Activation of the inside hind leg (in accordance with the canter) which is accentuated by the counter canter, will make the start of voltes, haunches in, much more simple later on, as well as normal pirouettes, as it is the inside hind leg which must be bent the most in order to bear the horse's mass pivoting around it.

The horse which is not capable of maintaining the correct lead in any position, or in any circumstance, cannot be said to be sufficiently in submission.

Counter canter will be useful later for exercises in higher dressage training.

When I begin the canter in place with any horse, I always begin by doing the counter canter on the outside track.

It is only much later, when the horse is straight and sure in the air, that I go on to a normal canter.

"The counter canter will assure us of a decisive strength in the horse." (Steinbrecht)

To resume: counter canter is an extraordinary method by which the hind legs can be activated at the canter, but care is needed to ensure that the horse does not become over tired at first as it is a violent exercise for him.

HAUNCHES-IN AT THE CANTER

Haunches-in at the canter is a precious exercise in order to make progress with the horse towards the collected canter.

On the other hand, it can be very dangerous when

badly done by an inexperienced rider who, by force, makes the croup move brusquely toward the inside, using his outside leg roughly.

Almost all riders who do this exercise abusively or tempestuously, use diagonal aids.

The croup moves inward in an effective way, but often to excess, when these aids are employed, passing in front of the shoulders in a tense fashion, while little hops of the hind legs can almost always be seen which do not correspond to the cantering action that the horse should maintain during this exercise.

What happens in the event of overdoing this exercise, or if it is used wrongly?

Crooked strike offs, by putting the haunches towards the interior will be one result. Also, the horse will lean inwards while doing flying changes instead of remaining straight, as is desirable.

If the croup is insufficiently mobile, it is due to the inside hind legs' lack of activity resulting from faulty gymnastic preparation, and the horse will start to resist, become heavy on the hand, and never produce a cantering stride which is really straight.

Let us now take a look at the method to use progressively in order to bring the horse to a point where he is able to canter in a haunches-in position. (Volte on two tracks at the canter).

If the strike offs at the canter are correct with the horse remaining straight along the wall, and if he does not lean to the outside, nor to the inside in a normal volte, his inside hind leg can start to be activated, little by little at the canter, while executing shoulder-in in a very large circle.

Judiciously employed, the rider's inside leg makes the horse enlarge the circle without changing the lead, or becoming disunited. The horse's entire mass starts to be displaced towards the outside. As soon as the horse obeys the rider's interior leg without resisting, while remaining calm and light, he should be made to advance his shoulders towards the interior of the circle, which becomes slowly smaller, by the use of lateral outside aids. The rider's inside leg must continue to act, but in moderation, during the exercise.

A direct rein will counterbalance the effect of the opposite rein, as it prevents the latter from turning the horse's head towards the outside, while supporting the shoulders.

If alternated, these two exercises, haunches-out and haunches-in, or in other terms, shoulder-in and volte on two tracks at the canter, should give the horse an extraordinary mobility and lightness at this gait.

The horse must be accustomed to go easily from one movement to the other, while cantering in a straight line.

Only after the horse can do all the preceding work effortlessly, can the volte on two tracks be made smaller in order to start the study of the pirouette.

I have tried to demonstrate that if gentleness and tact are used, little by little more results are achieved, not only in these latter exercises, but in all the dressage training of the horse, rather than by the use of violent aids. I am reminded of a passage from *L'Equitation des Dames* written by the Comte du Montigny, which goes as follows: "Permit us in closing, horsemen who read us, to tell you that the abusive use of immoderate and constant force is without effect, extinguishing and paralysing all efforts; in other words, this force leads to insensitivity and to complete indifference to the aids."

FLYING CHANGES AT THE CANTER

It is necessary to make a complete study of strike offs at the canter, practising them from the walk and from halts in order to completely understand and execute correct flying changes.

During the normal flying change, the inversion of the natural disposition of the hind legs begins as the inside fore leg is put down, and finishes during the time of suspension. The inversion of the fore legs' normal disposition begins during the time of suspension, continuing on during the descent and placing of the outside hind leg. For example, in the canter to the right, the legs go down in the following order: left hind leg, left diagonal, right fore leg.

At the moment when the right hind leg is put down, marking the first beat of the canter on the left lead, the flying change of the hind legs should occur.

The left hind leg should prolong its support, and its placement depends on that of its neighbour. The succession in the placement of the legs of the horse, constitutes the left canter: right hind leg, right diagonal, left fore leg.

Flying changes should not be started until the horse is calm in the canter, and can strike off from the walk on each hand with great ease.

Some horses quickly become calm and straight during flying changes without altering the canter's rhythm. Others have great difficulty when this exercise is demanded.

Each rider having a little tact and enough patience, while repudiating violence, can obtain flying changes quickly in the first case.

106

In the second, the problem must be resolved by great masters as it is one which takes a lot of time.

I have had to solve the difficulties of both types often.

I believe the system instituted by Fillis, found in *Principes de Dressage et d'Equitation* to be the best in order to train the horse in flying changes.

This consists of obtaining easy strike offs while straight, and in being able to maintain the counter canter. Then, a change from counter canter to normal canter may be demanded, being sure that the rider's leg, which will become the interior one, is active in the region of the girth in order to push the horse forwards.

When this becomes easy on each hand, start to ask for flying changes from the normal canter to the counter canter.

I believe this system to be more advisable to follow than that of General Decarpentry, found in his *l'Equitation Académique*, which consists of gradually diminishing the strides of the canter dispersed between each strike off from the walk, on both hands.

In the first system the flying change can be demanded without change of impulsion. In the second, this does not hold true.

I believe that, if the system of Fillis is practised with tact on a horse which has been properly prepared for the exercise, it will succeed.

Obviously, as I have already said above, there are exceptionally reticent horses who have difficulty in flying changes, and then only the great masters who have enormous experience, and virtuosity, can succeed in resolving this problem.

Procedures to obtain successive flying changes close together are no different. The important thing is the way in which the aids are used, the degree of preparation for the canter, and the position given to the horse.

FLYING CHANGES AT EVERY STRIDE

It is necessary to proceed calmly in order to come to the stage when flying changes at every stride may be demanded, after having ensured flying changes when asked for at every sixth, fifth, fourth, third and second stride. Only then, when the others are definite, should flying changes at every stride be tried. And only with a very light and flexible horse can they be done in the circle.

Almost any rider can make his horse do flying changes, more or less close together. Few can succeed in doing flying changes at every stride in the volte, serpentine, or in a figure of eight.

Flying changes at every stride are one of the most brilliant exercises of all the *Haute-Ecole* work.

Their merit lies in the conservation of the cadence in which the horse executes this air, in keeping a rigorously straight position, adjusted to the curve if necessary, and in the amplitude of stride at the moment of the change.

COLLECTED CANTER

This is the canter in which the horse is at his lightest, most mobile and most active, while completely subjugated to his rider's will.

The collected canter will become a canter in four beats time if it becomes more "seated", having the point of equilibrium in the hindquarters. The disassociation of the exterior diagonal operates with the descent and placing of the inside hind leg preceding that of the outside fore leg.

In spite of those who say that the canter should always be in three beats time, it is only possible to do pirouettes and the canter in place while cantering in four beats time.

This last has nothing in common with the canter of a drowsy or tired horse, who disassociates his exterior diagonal by placing his fore leg on the ground before his hind leg.

THE CANTER IN PLACE

This canter in four beats time is executed in a slowed down tempo, and the forehand is higher than in a normal canter.

If the horse does not detach each of his hind legs

109

properly, instead of canter in place, there is a series of small hops.

Canter in place is achieved by gradually diminishing the canter, and augmenting the collection, rather than by traction on the reins.

The canter in place is not obtained by merely sustaining impulsion, but by augmenting it in the measure of the reduction of speed in the gait. In this air, the horse must detach the hind legs properly from the ground. It is only then that he can shorten the canter enough to do this air, and also be able to go right into an extended, medium, or collected canter, without becoming disunited, nor altering the mechanics of the gaits.

It is difficult to obtain it correctly with regularity on each hand. This can only be done with a very light, well impulsioned, and above all, straight horse.

CANTER TO THE REAR

When the horse can do a canter in place easily, it is simple to make him canter to the rear.

The rider's legs, and slight seat movement will produce the canter to the rear, but never the hands.

The canter to the rear is a gait in which the horse backs very little, and very slowly, at every stride.

Collection would soon be lost if this were attempted by pulling on the reins. The hands' action would overload the

PLATE 15
Euclides in pirouette to the right at the canter

PLATE 16
Invincivel — levade

hind legs, and would prevent the conservation of mobility necessary to go backwards.

The horse must have an excellent constitution, a good back, and strong hocks to be considered a fit subject for this kind of training. Those who try to teach a weak horse this air are doomed to failure.

PIROUETTES AT THE CANTER

In order that the pirouette be judged correct, the horse must go into it in the rhythm of his canter, carrying out the entire pirouette in the same canter, and leaving it also in the same rhythm, which is the great difficulty of this exercise. It loses all its value when it is done with variations of cadence and rhythm by a horse who is unable to do a collected canter in four times.

A fast pirouette is relatively easy to do, and is called a tornado (*tourbillon*).

I believe that if the horse knows how to canter in place it is much easier to start the pirouettes.

As preparatory work it is necessary to teach the horse how to do pirouettes at an extremely collected walk.

THE SCHOOL LEVADE

The classical levade is a preparation for other airs, such as the courbette, the ballotade, and the capriole.

Only when the horse has attained a high degree of dressage training, is steady, and can remain very collected, can he begin the airs above the ground (*airs relevés*) and the school jumps (*sauts d'école*).

When the horse can do a good piaffer with reinforced flexion of the haunches, he is finally ready to be considered as a fit subject for the teaching of the levade or the pesade.

In order for the horse to do a good levade, the gymnastic training of the haunches must have been attentively carried out in a methodical fashion, as otherwise the horse could only keep his fore legs in the air for a few seconds.

The fore legs' height and stability in the air, rigorously joined at the same height, constitutes the air that is a start towards the preparation for school jumps. This air is the levade or pesade.

The horse's hind legs, which must be nearly in a sitting position with the feet well forward under the horse's body, support the weight of the horse and rider.

The angle made by the horse's body and the ground should be at 30° to 45°.

The fore legs should be bent at the knees, while the cannons should be as close as possible to the forearms.

The horse should be pushed against the bit in the air, but without force.

If the horse starts to back, refusing to go on to the bit, or flexes his neck over much (*s'encapuchonner*), even if his forehand leaves the ground during the levade, it is a sign of sourness and resistance in the horse as he refuses to execute the air correctly, with impulsion and real collection.

In such a case, the horse must be pushed ahead by the use of energetic aids, and asked for the piaffer with a high foreleg action, well collected, and well pressed into the rider's hands.

In the levade, as in all the school airs, the horse himself will indicate to the rider what position and attitude that the latter should adopt. It is necessary that the rider balance his weight evenly and correctly which will lead the horse to do the same.

The hindlegs of the horse must be placed under the horse's body by means of the rider's legs and spurs when the levade is demanded; when this is realised, judicious help by the rider's hand makes the forehand rise as the weight is brought back on to the hind legs.

As soon as the levade has been obtained, the rider's hands have nothing to do other than maintain contact with the horse's mouth. If the weight shows a tendency to go forwards, help stabilise the horse with the hands so that the horse is again in a good position during the levade, and then give way in the fingers when this has been obtained.

The important thing is to maintain contact with the horse's mouth.

If there is too much weight resting on the hock, slight pressure of the rider's leg will be remedy enough.

In order that the horse can come down from this air, and put his fore legs on the ground, the rider's hands must yield little by little as they regulate the descent of the forehand.

Characteristic of a good levade is the gentleness with which the horse begins and finishes that air, and the

115

promptness with which he moves ahead after finishing it.

Training horses of uncertain temperament and little impulsion in the levade is not advisable, as with these horses many months of previous training risks being lost.

Nor are lessons in that air to be counselled for horses with weak hocks. They will never have the brilliance that a strong horse has, and on the contrary, they will be ruined.

Only horses who are well made, strong, with solid hocks, a strong croup, and who are naturally full of impulsion, can and should be trained in that air and in other airs above the ground.

The levade will be really brilliant if the training has been well conducted, with haunches well bent, gymnastically trained, and remaining bent at the piaffer, at the school canter, in the pirouettes, and when descending after a levade.

I believe that anyone wishing to study the subject in depth, should, after reading the books of the great masters who did these airs so well, analyse the engravings of the period. The noble attitudes depicted in these engravings bear little resemblance to what we see nowadays. The attitude of the horse who rises high rapidly, with the hind legs spreading out behind him, and without the slightest collection, has nothing in common with the school levade. In fact, it is nothing but an exploitation of the horse's action when resisting the rider. I believe that dismounted work may be carried out in the levade on the longe rein without having to have recourse to the pillars. Done with care, the result will be equally brilliant.

BRILLIANCE

By useful gymnastics, the horse may be made to shine
with brilliance in such a way, coupled with the correct
position of the rider, that a vision of great beauty will be
seen by the spectator.

If the horse has been initiated into the airs of the *Haute-
Ecole* calmly, without annoyances, when it is necessary to
give him better action, and to ask for more brilliance it will
be possible without efforts or resistance.

Exercises carried out by means of sharp spurs and harsh
bits will not obtain beauty and grace from the horse. The
more that the horse is pushed, the more his fire becomes
extinguished. The hallmark of good dressage training,
which is ease and dexterity, will be taken from him.

Sans Pareil, a horse ridden by Commandant Rousselet
worked so happily and freely during Cadre Noir exhibitions,
that he gave little hops from gaiety.

Try, for example, to start the piaffer by leg action alone,
and then one day, if you touch the horse with the spurs,
you will see that he appears to have sprouted wings.

Several years ago, I gave up using spurs with rowels. I
ride all horses without them, whether they be lax, or with
hot blood, or whether they be sweet tempered or irritable.
I have had much more satisfying results than when I rode
with rowelled spurs.

What is essential is not to tighten the legs during the
dressage training, but rather to use them without effort
while allowing them to hang softly near the horse's sides.

Even when using the spur with intensity, the leg action must be soft and relaxed.

In order to use the legs in this fashion, it is necessary to have a very good position while mounted, having complete independence between the aids and unification with the horse while accompanying his movements, never going against him.

Only a tranquil rider, who has soft and discreet aids is capable of riding a really trained horse.

If the effort of the rider is apparent to the spectator, despite pretensions to the contrary, the value in terms of *Haute-Ecole* is nil.

Classic and academic equitation is not a spectacle which is lassitudinous and dull. It is a calm and serene spectacle in which the horse may be seen to have pleasure.

As it may not be well understood, in concluding, I must again emphasise that artistic development obtained by superior techniques must go hand in hand with the rider's tact and feeling, and in the quality of physical and moral decontraction shown by his horse, which makes possible a great interpretation of equestrian art.

Sadly enough this art is fugitive, as once the horse is dead, nothing, not even films, can reproduce the sensation felt when the horse is seen in movement. Death eradicates all the work of the artist, unlike musical scores or paintings which live on to lend immortality to their creator. After the horse is no more, only those who have admired him keep a remembrance of his quality in their hearts, which is gradually effaced by Time, and others who have not seen him know him only by romanticised tales, recounted, and sometimes embroidered, by those who have truly loved him.

Readers of this book who wish to be informed about new and forthcoming publications on horses and horsemanship, are invited to send their name and address to:

J. A. Allen & Company Limited,
1, Lower Grosvenor Place,
Buckingham Palace Road,
London, SW1W 0EL.